The Relational God

A 10-Session Bible Study Leader's Guide

What the Bible Says about Our Identities As:
Sons and Daughters
Husbands and Wives
Brothers and Sisters
Fathers and Mothers
How Those Relationships Thrive
and What They Teach Us about God

Steven J. Halbert

The Relational God Bible Study Leader's Guide: What the Bible Says about Our Identities as Sons and Daughters, Husbands and Wives, Brothers and Sisters, Fathers and Mothers—How Those Relationships Thrive and What They Teach Us about God

Copyright © 2020 by Steven J. Halbert

Published by Tusitala Publishers, 206 Sassafras Drive; Taylors, SC 29687

All rights reserved. No part of this publication may be reproduced without the prior permission of the publisher, except as provided for by US copyright law.

Cover design: Steven J. Halbert
Cover image: Aunt Kitty

Edited by: Steven J. Halbert

Fillable PDF by: Steven J. Halbert

Printed in the United States of America, First Printing 2020

Scripture quotations, unless otherwise noted, are from ESV® Bible (The Holy Bible, English Standard Version®), copyright © 2001 by Crossway, a publishing ministry of Good News Publishers. Used by permission. All rights reserved. Scripture marked KJV is taken from the King James Version of the Bible. Scripture quotations marked NIV are taken from the Holy Bible, New International Version®, NIV® Copyright ©1973, 1978, 1984, 2011 by Biblica, Inc.® Used by permission. All rights reserved worldwide. Scripture quotations marked (NASB) taken from the New American Standard Bible® (NASB), Copyright © 1960, 1962, 1963, 1968, 1971, 1972, 1973, 1975, 1977, 1995 by The Lockman Foundation Used by permission. www.Lockman.org.

Trade paperback ISBN: 978-0-9993099-8-8
PDF ISBN: 978-0-9993099-9-5

Library of Congress Cataloging-in-Publication Data

Names: Halbert, Steven Joseph, 1983- author.
Title: The Relational God Bible Study Leader's Guide: What the Bible Says about Our Identities as Sons and Daughters, Husbands and Wives, Brothers and Sisters, Fathers and Mothers–How Those Relationships Thrive and What They Teach Us about God
Description: Greenville: Tusitala Publishers, 2020.
Library of Congress Control Number: 2019904661

Hello

I'm excited that you have chosen to teach *The Relational God Bible Study*. It will be a challenging but rewarding curriculum to teach.

Whether you are a new teacher or a seasoned facilitator, *The Relational God Bible Study* provides plenty of content for you to work through with your group. In the following pages, I have compiled a resource to help you navigate the curriculum. There are numerous ways to teach this content, but I would suggest one of two:

1. The companion Bible study workbook contains reading assignments and "Key Concepts" to look for while reading. It has been my experience that people do not typically read assignments during the week. Therefore, I have created a teaching outline of the content of the applicable reading in the pages below. The "Key Concept" questions are in bold. The teaching outline will not make much sense outside of thorough reading of the applicable chapter(s). Use the outline to reinforce and structure the primary concepts.
2. The companion Bible study also contains two summary tables of the content. I have repeated these tables three pages over. These tables provide the "Key Concepts" and primary Scripture references for each section. More experienced teachers may just want to take this information and build a lesson off the concepts and Scriptures each week.

Again, there are multiple ways to go about teaching the content, so if you find something that is helpful to you, run with it.

Just remember that the **primary purpose** of the Bible study is to examine **what Scripture commands for each of the relationships,** and **what that reveals** to us **about the nature and character of God**.

I try to repeat that about once each session, so that the class doesn't lose sight of it. Whenever you begin discussing relationships, it is very easy to forget the primary purpose.

My goal in writing this curriculum was to help people see what the Bible says for each of their God-created relationships. Too many times I think we become anxious about things that are not necessarily biblical. They may be good, but they are not primary. This Bible study is an attempt to examine what is biblically required for each of the relationships considered.

My heart's desire is that the Word of God would be primary in our relationships. There is plenty of Scripture to examine throughout the curriculum, so please try to stick to Scripture throughout the study:

> For the word of God is living and active, sharper than any two-edged sword, piercing to the division of soul and of spirit, of joints and of marrow, and discerning the thoughts and intentions of the heart. (Hebrews 4:12)

From a content perspective, each lesson (except for the Introductory Lesson) is laid out in the same way:

- **Big Idea** – the main theme of the session.
- **Key Scripture** – the primary Scripture(s) to be reviewed for that session.
- **Read** – the corresponding chapter(s) to read prior to the group session.
- **Key Concepts** – questions to answer while you read.
- **Community Study and Discussion** – material to facilitate discussion and application of the key concepts.

This Leader's Guide contains some additional content to help you facilitate the class. The content in the Leader's Guide is laid out as follows:

- **Bridge** – a statement designed to shift focus from the previous session's content to the current session's content.
- **Big Idea** – the main theme of the session.
- **Key Scripture** – the primary Scripture(s) to be reviewed for that session (note that these might be different from what is in the Bible Study).
- **Read** – the corresponding chapter(s) to read prior to the group session.
- **Preparation** – some questions and ideas to help you dig deeper into the content as you prepare to facilitate or teach.
- **Intro Questions** – questions to prompt discussion in your class before you dive into the "Community Study and Discussion" content.
- **Teaching Outline** – if you choose to do more than just go through the "Community Study and Discussion" questions with your group each week, this section outlines the key points from the chapter. I have put the questions from the "Key Concepts" portion of the workbook in bold, as well as any Scripture references used.
- **Digging Deeper and Additional Resources** – Some ideas for going deeper in the content or developing your Bible study skills (these are at the end of each "Section" (so located at the end of Sessions 3, 6, 7, 9, and 10).

As you read along in the book, you will notice that the Bible study largely ignores the first chapter of each section. The first chapter of each section in the book is used to identify our own personal experiences and illustrate that the Bible contains stories of people who don't get it right, but whom God still uses.

This can be helpful to teach through, but I feel the primary application comes from looking at what Scripture commands us to apply in our lives. Indeed, when you are comfortable doing so, don't be afraid to open up and identify areas where you personally struggle in relationships. This will encourage further openness within the group.

You may also notice that the **Key Scriptures** are different in the Bible Study vs. the Leader's Guide. The **Key Scriptures** in the Bible Study are generally Scriptures that are referenced in the **Community Study and Discussion** or were very important from the reading. The **Key Scriptures** in the Leader's Guide are Scriptures that are referenced in bold on the **Teaching Outline**. If the Scripture is not in bold on the outline, then it is mostly just reference.

It is my prayer that God will use this material to transform the lives and hearts of the participants, improve their family relationships, their relationships with their brothers and sisters in Christ, and their relationship with God.

Grace and Peace,

--Steven J. Halbert

THEMES			
	Biblical Commands	**Us to God**	**God**
Child	• Honor • Obey • Learn	• Shifting Dependence • Spiritual Maturity • We Are God's Children	• Jesus as the Son of God
Spouse	• Wives–Submit • Husbands–Love • Husbands – Leave and Hold Fast • Physical Intimacy • Faithfulness • Misc. Commands	• Christ and the Church • The Spiritual Covenant	• The Godhead
Sibling	• Warnings • Unity • Greeting • Support/Prayer • Equity	• Bros. & Sis. w/Christ (vertical) • Bros. & Sis. In Christ (horizontal)	• Jesus the Firstborn among Many Brothers
Parent	• Teach/Model • Discipline • Gentleness • Love	• Spiritual Parenting • Teaching & Modeling • Discipline • Prayer & Generosity	• God as father • Mother Heart of God • Jesus as Son of God

REFERENCES			
	Biblical Commands	**Us to God**	**God**
Child	• Exodus 20:12 • Luke 2:41–52 • Ephesians 6:1–3	• Romans 8:14–17, 29 • Galatians 3:15–4:7 • Hebrews 5:12–14; 12:3–11 • 1 John 2:12–14	• John 1:1–4, 14 • John 3:14–17
Spouse	• 1 Corinthians 7 • Ephesians 5:15–33 • Colossians 3:19 • 1 Peter 3:7 • Titus 2:3–5	• Luke 14:26 • Romans 12:4–8 • 1 Corinthians 12 • Ephesians 5:22–32 • Revelation 19:6–9; 21:4, 9–11	• John 15:1–17 • Romans 7:1–6 • Colossians 1:15–20
Sibling	• Matthew 5:22–24; 7:3–5 • Romans 1:11–13; 15:25–30; 16:14 • 2 Thessalonians 3:15 • 1 John 2:9–11; 3:10–16; 4:20–21	• Mark 10:29–30 • Romans 8:14–17, 29 • Hebrews 2:5–3:6	• N/A
Parent	• Deuteronomy 6:4–9 • Proverbs 13:24; 19:18 • Ephesians 6:4 • Titus 2:4	• Matthew 7:7–11; 28:19 • John 15:12–16 • Romans 8:15 • Hebrews 12:5–10	• John 15:12–16 • Colossians 1:15 • Titus 3:3–7 • James 3:17–18

Session 1 – Introduction

- **Bridge:** Welcome to *The Relational God Bible Study*. The goal of this study is to examine what God's Word commands for our relationships as children, spouses, siblings, and parents. After discovering the commands for these relationships, we will explore what they teach us about the nature and character of God. So, let's dive in and take some time to get to know one another and talk about why we're here.

- **Big Idea:** God could have created us to be in any sort of relationships that He wanted, yet He created us to be children, spouses, siblings, and parents in order to reveal something about His nature and character.

- **Key Scripture:** Ephesians 5:21–6:4

- **Read:** Introduction of *The Relational God*

- **Preparation:**
    - Read through "Session 1 – Introduction" in the Bible study
    - Read through the "Introduction" in *The Relational God*.
        - Consider telling your own story in a similar manner.
        - Consider how you can get your class to think about their own stories and relational histories.
    - Read Ephesians 5–6 to get a context for the Key Scripture

- **Intro Question(s)**
    - What has been your most challenging familial relationship?
    - Your most rewarding familial relationship?
    - Why?
    - Asked differently, what has been the biggest hinderance or the biggest help to one of your familial relationships? If a specific event is mentioned, try to get to the heart issue (i.e. if someone says, "when so-and-so lied to me," link that to "trust").

- **Teaching Outline**
    - Review Session 1 together
        - Format (possibly discuss timing, how long reading and completing the study will take each week)
        - Clearly articulate the goal and themes of the study
            - **What are the four physical relationships specifically established by God?** Child, Spouse, Sibling, and Parent
            - **God could have made us to be in any sort of relationships. Why those?** When these relationships are practiced biblically, they reflect something that God wants us to know about His nature and character
    - Facilitate Community Study and Discussion
        - **Of the God-given relationships (the relationships specifically established by God), which do you think could use the most work in your life? Why?** Personal application, answers will differ
        - **What is at least one thing you would like to see improved in each of these relationships?** Personal application, answers will differ
        - **What else are you hoping to get out of this study (why are you here)?** Personal application, answers will differ

- **Additional Time? Pray for One Another, Plan Service Project, Fellowship!**

Final Page(s) for Sketching, Doodling, or Additional Thoughts / Notes

Final Page(s) for Sketching, Doodling, or Additional Thoughts / Notes

Session 2 – How to Be a Child

- **Bridge:** Over the next few weeks, we will be examining what the Bible commands for each of these relationships and what doing these relationships well tells us about the nature and character of God. We'll start with the one relationship that affects all of us. We are all children.

- **Big Idea:** children are to honor, obey, and learn from their parents; and the goal of childhood is to shift dependence from our parents and onto _____.

- **Key Scripture:** Exodus 20:12 | Luke 2:41–52 | Ephesians 6:1–3

- **Read:** Chapters 1 and 2 of *The Relational God*

- **Preparation:**
    - Read the entirety of Exodus chapter 20. Why do you think the command in Exodus 20:12 makes the list?
    - Contrast Exodus 20:12 with Ephesians 6:1–3. What do you notice? What is the same? What are the differences?
    - Read the entirety of Ephesians chapter 5 and 6. How does the context help clarify the command to children?
    - Read Deuteronomy 6:4–9. What does God command His people to do with His commands? How does He tell His people to do that?

- **Intro Question(s)**
    - Think about being a child (not from a parent's perspective). Try to remember life as a child. What stands out? What do you remember?
    - What is the goal of childhood?

The Relational God Bible Study Leader's Guide

- **Teaching Outline**
  - Review the questions in the "Personal Study" section with the class.
  - Let's look first at what the Bible commands children.
    - **Exodus 20:12** – honor
      - This is in a list to *everyone* (including adults).
      - **What does it mean to honor?**
      - Hebrew *kabad* – assigning value (high value).
    - **Ephesians 6:1–3** – obey (and honor)
      - Paul uses the Exodus passage in Ephesians. The Greek term he uses for *honor* also has economic implications. It is about assigning value to something monetarily.
      - Ethos, pathos, logos – you cannot be neutral about something that is honored.
      - This is in a passage directed towards Christian households (see these are children who are young in age).
      - Paul adds *obey*. So, at a minimum, honor for younger children includes obedience.
      - The word for obey is *hupakouō*.
        - It means *under the hearing*.
        - In order for you to *obey* someone, then, they must have a natural and/or legal authority to command your obedience. Parents certainly have that in regards to children.
        - **So when does this stop? When do we no longer have to obey?**
  - **Jesus models** for us **what the goal of childhood is**, and, in doing so, also answers the question, **when do we no longer have to obey?** Let's look at **Luke 2:41–52**.
    - Is Jesus obedient to His parents in this passage? Why not?
    - What word does the passage use concerning Jesus' posture towards His parents after this incident (v. 51)?
    - Thus the goal of childhood is a shift in dependence.
  - There is one more command in Scripture to children, and it is that they learn (**Deuteronomy 6:4–9; Proverbs 1:8; Proverbs 4:1–9**). **How are children to learn?**
    - Life lessons – circumstantial

- **Additional Time? Pray for One Another, Plan Service Project, Fellowship!**

Final Page(s) for Sketching, Doodling, or Additional Thoughts / Notes

Final Page(s) for Sketching, Doodling, or Additional Thoughts / Notes

Session 3 – Sons and Daughters of God

- **Bridge:** So, if the goal of childhood is to shift dependence, then somehow these commands must be able to help us do that? Let's think about how we do that spiritually.

- **Big Idea:** we are the sons and daughters of God (through Christ); therefore, we need to grow up in the Lord.

- **Key Scripture:** Psalm 1:3 | Proverbs 1:7 | John 15 | Romans 8:14–17, 29; 10:13 Colossians 1:15–18 | Hebrews 5:12–14; 12:3–11 | 1 Peter 2:1–3 | 1 John 2:12–14

- **Read:** Chapter 3 of *The Relational God*

- **Preparation:**
    - What are the four stages of spiritual development according to 1 John 2:12–14? Summarize them in your own words (my summary is at the end of the outline).
    - Do you recall how you move from one stage to the next? If you need help, go back and look at 1 Peter 2:1–3 and Hebrews 12:3–11; 5:12–14. Summarize that in your own words.
    - One of the ways that we move through these stages of development is by abiding in Christ. Read John 15:1–17. List some ways that you might abide in Christ.

- **Intro Question(s)** – What do the physical commands to children teach us about how we should interact as sons and daughters of God?

- **Teaching Outline**
  - Review the questions in the "Personal Study" section with the class.
  - Let's look at **Romans 8:14–17, 29**
    - **The role of Christ and our position as children of God**.
      - We are considered sons and daughters of God in the first place because of Christ.
        - We are adopted (v. 15)
        - We have intimacy with the Father (v. 15)
      - We are "fellow heirs" (v. 17)
      - He is the "firstborn among many brothers" (v. 29)
    - **So how do we become children of God?** Let's look at **Romans 10:13. Have you done that?**
  - If we are children of God, then we need to grow up in the Lord.
    - Let's take a look at **1 John 2:12–14. What stages of spiritual development do you see? What characterizes each?**
      - Little Children – sins are forgiven (salvation)
        - New believer. A spiritual "infant."
        - Has accepted Christ but has not done much else in their spiritual life.
      - Children – know the Father (growing in knowledge)
        - Has moved beyond just salvation.
        - Has begun learning (taking in knowledge).
        - Is receiving discipline / mentoring from the church and other sources.
      - Young Men (Young Adult) – strong, Word of God abides in you, and you have overcome the evil one (2x)
        - Has begun internalizing what is being learned.
        - Is beginning to be self-disciplined (i.e. is not needing to be spoon-fed as much as they are beginning to seek out spiritual growth on their own).
        - They are gaining spiritual strength.
        - They are experiencing victory in spiritual warfare.
        - They are distinguishing between good and evil.
        - They are able to teach (beginning to disciple others).

- Fathers (Parent) – know Him who is from the beginning (2x)
  - They have spiritually reproduced.
  - They are bringing people to Christ and actively involved in discipling others.
  - They are rooted in the Lord, and their roots run deep (Psalm 1).
  - They cast out fear and live in love (1 John 4:18) – i.e. it is not easy to shake their faith. They have embraced the truth of Romans 8:38-39 (that nothing shall be able to separate them from the love of God in Christ Jesus our Lord).
- Where do you think our culture tends to get stuck (both physically and spiritually)?
- Let's spend some time drilling down and focusing on young men (young adult).
  - How do we move from being a spiritual "child" to being a spiritual "young man" (young adult)?
    - First John tells us that young men "overcome the evil one," they are "strong," and the "Word of God abides in them."
    - Let's also consider what Hebrews 5:12-14 says about young men (they "ought to be teachers," they have "trained themselves," and they are able to "distinguish good from evil").
  - So how do we develop these things? How do we progress?
    - Foundation is abiding
      - John 15 uses "abide" 15x times!
      - What is the result of abiding (v. 5)?
      - Moving from a spiritual child to a spiritual youth requires *abiding*. Start here. Meditate on this.
      - Abiding requires shifting dependence from parents or self to God

- Next let's consider self-discipline, teaching, and discernment
    o Hebrews 5 tells us that young men have "trained themselves" (or "trained by constant practice" ESV). This is self-discipline. But before you can get to self-discipline, you need to receive regular discipline.
    o Let's consider **Hebrews 12:3–11**
        - The word for *discipline* here is *paideuō*. Anyone recognize this word? It is a word that indicates someone being trained by someone else. Children are still being trained by someone else (and we are always children . . . we always have something to *learn*).
        - The word has at its root *disciple*. It has the connotation of mentoring. Its why we *abide*.
        - Yet the word in Hebrews 5:14 is different. The word for "train" is *gymnazio*. This is when the discipline received through abiding becomes your own. You don't "need someone to teach you." You are doing it yourself!
        - **So, the difference between *discipline* and *train* is that "discipline" (*paideuō*) indicates that you are being helped along, mentored. "Train" (*gymnazio*) indicates that you are actively pursuing growth on your own.**
    o Now the cycle completes, because now you can teach others. You can help others *abide*. You can *disciple* others! You are *teaching*.
    [if self-discipline terminates on the self, it dies on the vine–you need to help run the gym]
    o There is one piece left. *Discernment*. Let's look at **Proverbs 1:7** (which mirrors the stages of development we are talking about)
        - Beginning of knowledge – infant
        - Knowledge (v. 1:3) – child
        - Wisdom and Instruction – young men
        - Discernment – actively working towards wise choices being made.

- There's one final stage that John mentions in 1 John 2:12–14. Let's briefly examine this final stage of "Fathers."
  - Fathers "know him who is from the beginning."
  - It has a totality that includes the other stages and is spread across all aspects of life. Consider **Colossians 1:15–18**.
  - Fathers have the rootedness of a vine that has *abided* for a long time. It is reminiscent of **Psalm 1:3**.
    - Fathers have passed through the stages of "young man."
      - They have been discipled
      - They have developed self-discipline
      - They have taught and built up the kingdom (spiritually reproduced)
      - They have discernment
    - Fathers abide with Christ. They are *rooted* (and the roots go deep)
      - The storms, tests, and trials of this life do not cause his leaf to wither.
      - Because of this rootedness and *dependence*, he prospers in all that he does.
      - The father is the successful child.

- **Additional Time? Pray for One Another, Plan Service Project, Fellowship!**

- **Digging Deeper and Additional Resources for Sessions 2 and 3:**
  - In chapter 1 of *The Relational God,* you saw me apply some of these principles to Joseph, Jesus, and the Prodigal Son.
    - Consider trying this yourself.
    - Think about another biblical character's childhood. What do you notice about how they follow (or don't follow) the biblical commands to children?
  - Read Brother Lawrence's *Practicing the Presence of God*
  - Read Charles Swindoll's *Intimacy with the Almighty*

  - Watch Star Wars Episode 1, 2, or 3, and listen out for our word for *discipline*

The Relational God Bible Study Leader's Guide

- Contrast what you have learned about the stages of development with the parable of the sower in Matthew 13. What do you notice? How would you categorize the different seed with the different stages of development?
- Read the book of Proverbs in the Bible
    - Consider marking all the instructions to children found in the book
    - Before or after reading explore it using The Bible Project (https://thebibleproject.com/explore/proverbs/)
- Read *The Discipline of Spiritual Discernment* by Tim Challies
- Read the section on the Hypostatic Union in Wayne Grudem's *Systematic Theology*

Final Page(s) for Sketching, Doodling, or Additional Thoughts / Notes

Final Page(s) for Sketching, Doodling, or Additional Thoughts / Notes

Session 4 – How to Be a Spouse I

- **Bridge:** Now that we have examined how we *approach* God (as children) by shifting dependency *from* parents *to* God, we will consider how we *interact* with God individually and corporately as the church (like a spouse) and what that tells us about the nature and character of God.

- **Big Idea:** In biblical marriage, both spouses are called to physical intimacy and faithfulness. Husbands specifically are called to love their wives; leave childhood; and live with their wives in gentleness, understanding, and honor. Wives specifically are called to love and submit to their husbands, be self-controlled, pure, kind, and keep the home.

- **Key Scripture:** Genesis 3:16 | Ephesians 5:1–2, 15–33 | Philippians 2:5–8

- **Read:** Chapters 4 and 5 of *The Relational God*

- **Preparation:**
    - Read the book of Ephesians and Philippians 2, pay specific attention to how Christ treats the church and how the church treats Christ.
    - How does Ephesians 5 start (vv. 1–2)?
    - What is the responsibility of all believers? (vv. 3–21)

- **Notice that the Community Study for the next two sessions is broken into a section for men and a section for women.**

- **Intro Question(s)**
    - Think back to your wedding day. How has marriage been different than you imagined (better or more difficult)?
    - How have other family relationships affected your marriage (children, parents, siblings)?

- **Teaching Outline**
  - Review the questions in the "Personal Study" section with the class.
  - We're going to primarily be in **Ephesians 5:15–33** for this lesson. What does this passage say to:
    - Husbands (love and leave parents and hold fast to wife)
    - Wives (submit)
  - Let's flesh this out a bit. First, look at **Ephesians 5:1–2, 21**.
    - **What is the context for the commands we're about to review?**
      - Our attitude should be that of Christ (v. 2)
      - We are to submit to one another (v. 21)
  - So with that context in mind, let's look at the **primary command to wives in the Ephesians passage: submission**.
    - **Difference between (*hupakouō* and *hupatassō*):**
      - *Hupakouō* – obey (automatically under authority)
      - *Hupotassō* – submit (placed under authority)
    - This is also only within the marital relationship (i.e. it is not all women to all men), nor is it indicative of status.
    - Furthermore, this is to be a picture of the church. How does the church submit to Christ?
  - Now let's look at the **primary commands to husbands in the Ephesians passage: love**
    - Giving up the self (5:25b) – consider **Philippians 2:5–8**
    - Sanctifying her (5:26a)
    - Cleansing her with the washing of the Word (5:26b)
    - Presenting to Himself in splendor (5:27a)
    - For the purpose of her holiness (5:27b)
    - Loving as you love the self (5:28)
    - Nourishing and cherishing her (5:29)
  - There's one final command to men in the Ephesians passage (vv. 31–32)
    - It begins in Genesis 2:24 (before there are even parents)
    - It comes after the part about sacrificial love, but before the part about physical intimacy
    - It provides breathing room for the marriage
    - It is on the husband to lead forward in creating this new family
    - Genesis 3:6 shows that men tend toward passivity (Adam let her eat the fruit . . . he let her be the guinea pig for sin)

- o The curse, just a few verses later, shows us **why – in the created order – these commands might be in place**. This was perhaps illustrated by a translation change in Genesis 3:16 that has happened within our lifetime (this content is in chapter 6, but I cover it here when teaching – for the sake of time):
    - 2011 – "Your desire shall be *for* your husband, *and* he shall rule over you"
    - 2016 – "Your desire shall be *contrary to* your husband, *but* he shall rule over you"
    - These seem almost opposites, but when you think about it in light of what did not change ("he shall rule over you"), the implication is the same.
        - In the first instance, the temptation of the wife is emphasized.
        - In the second instance, the temptation of the husband is emphasized.
        - In the first instance the husband is viewed as ruling over the wife—taking advantage of her desire.
        - In the second instance, the wife is viewed as desiring the role of the husband—being disappointed in his leadership.
        - Thus, the temptation to sin for the wife is a lack of submission.
        - And, the temptation to sin for the husband is an unloving, authoritarian rule.
        - Husbands, love requires gentle leadership, and the first step in that gentle leadership is for us to "leave [our] father and mother" to form a new family (and this comes before the "becoming one" of physical intimacy).
- o A word about roles: it is not your job to make your husband love or make your wife submit. **You worry about the commands given to you**.

- **Additional Time? Pray for One Another, Plan Service Project, Fellowship!**

The Relational God Bible Study Leader's Guide

19

Final Page(s) for Sketching, Doodling, or Additional Thoughts / Notes

Final Page(s) for Sketching, Doodling, or Additional Thoughts / Notes

Final Page(s) for Sketching, Doodling, or Additional Thoughts / Notes

Session 5 – How to Be a Spouse II

- **Bridge:** Last session we began looking at the commands specific to each spouse in Ephesians 5. This session we'll conclude our examination of Ephesians 5 and then move into some other commands in Scripture that should be shaping our marriages.

- **Big Idea:** In biblical marriage, both men and women need to be committed to faithfulness and physical intimacy. Husbands, specifically need to leave and hold fast, love, and live with their wife in gentleness, understanding, and honor. Wives specifically need to submit to, love, and live with their husbands in self-control, purity, and kindness

- **Key Scripture:** Genesis 1:27 | Psalm 66:18 | 1 Corinthians 6:16–20; 7:1–5 Ephesians 5:15–33 | Colossians 3:19 | Titus 2:3–5 | 1 Peter 3:7

- **Read:** Chapter 6 of *The Relational God*

- **Preparation:**
    - Set aside some time this week to discuss your marriage with your spouse. What is working well? What isn't? Discuss some of the content from last week's lesson. Ask specifically how you are doing on your part (without aiming to provide feedback about he or she is doing on his or her part).
    - During the Community Study and Discussion, I focus on the primary commands to husband and wives; however, it might be a good idea to bring out the other two commands for both spouses which this chapter covers (physical intimacy and faithfulness).

- **Notice that the Community Study for the next two sessions is broken into a section for men and a section for women.**

- **Intro Question(s):** Did anyone have conversations with their spouses that they would like to share?

- **Teaching Outline**
  - Review the questions in the "Personal Study" section with the class.
  - **The two primary commands to which both husbands and wives are to adhere is physical intimacy and faithfulness.**
  - Everything up to this point has been rooted in the Ephesians 5 passage. Now we will move on to other passages and concepts. The first is **faithfulness**
    - Harder to see, because there is no explicit command, nor can faithfulness be demonstrated with solitary action
    - God is referred to most often as "faithful" in the Psalms
    - Book of Hosea
    - Matthew 19:3–11
  - **Physical Intimacy**
    - Let's not pull any punches. According to the Ephesians passage, "becoming one" is meant to be a picture of Christ's union with the church!
    - So, what else does the Bible say about sex that can better help us understand not only ourselves, but also that for which God designed this relationship
    - **Genesis 1:27** – the mingling of souls that occurs when these two become one takes the image of God in both male and female and unites them into one image.
      - This is why sex should be saved for marriage. It is like separating a bit of your soul into the other person.
      - **1 Corinthians 6:16–20** illustrates further the gravity of such an act.
    - The husband and wife are on equal footing sexually **1 Corinthians 7:1–5**
      - A spouse is God's good and perfect gift for our sexual desire
      - We are to serve our spouse with our body, but **we are not to blame our spouse for our inability to remain pure.**
  - **Additionally Husbands** – **Colossians 3:19** and **1 Peter 3:7** tells men to **live with their wives with gentleness, understanding, and honor**.
    - To some extent this is an extension of *love*.
    - There is a **consequence** and it is congruent with **Psalm 66:18**. Being understanding with our wives, valuing them, and not being harsh with them are **prerequisites for our prayers being heard**.

- - - **Wives** – **Titus 2:3–5** tells wives to **love their husbands to be self-controlled, pure, working at home, and kind**.
      - The love mentioned in this passage is different than the love mentioned in Ephesians (for the men), and we will get to that in the section on parenting. For now, just realize that the love in this passage has a certain tangible quality to it. Thus, **men are to love their wives unconditionally and women are to love their husbands (and children) in tangible ways** [that must be taught]. [also, interestingly enough, we often reverse this].
        - Being self-controlled, pure, working at home, and kind are tangible expressions of this sort of love.
        - Like the commands for the men, there is a **consequence** for not doing these. **The Word of God is reviled**.
  - **Conclusion (and to review)**:
    - The Commands of Marriage – how to be a spouse
      - **Both:**
        - Physical Intimacy
        - Faithfulness
      - **Men:**
        - Leave and Hold Fast
        - Love
        - Gentleness, Understanding, and Honor
      - **Women:**
        - Submission
        - Love, Self-Control, Purity, Keeping the Home, and Kindness
    - **Marriages that do these things well reflect a greater picture**, but the opposite is also true (with literally damming results).
      - Submission without love is control on the husband's part and slavery on the wife's part. Hell on earth
      - Love without submission is juvenility on the wife's part and abuse toward the husband. Hell on earth.
      - Scripture begins and ends with a wedding. Adam and Eve and all of our marriages are painting a picture of that final wedding at the end of time. It is the marriage of the Lamb to His bride, the church. And what is the opposite of this end time marriage feast? Is it not quite literally hell? **Thus our marriages can quite literally be pictures of heaven or hell.**
- **Additional Time? Pray for One Another, Plan Service Project, Fellowship!**

Final Page(s) for Sketching, Doodling, or Additional Thoughts / Notes

Final Page(s) for Sketching, Doodling, or Additional Thoughts / Notes

Final Page(s) for Sketching, Doodling, or Additional Thoughts / Notes

Session 6 – Christ and the Church

- **Bridge:** Whenever we discuss the commands for marriage, it is easy to become discouraged. Most of our marriages are not where we would like them to be. That is why the commands are so important, though, because our marriages were meant to reflect something beautiful. Christ's relationship with His bride, the church.

- **Big Idea:** Our marriages are designed to reflect the relationship of Christ and the church, the Godhead, and our spiritual covenant

- **Key Scripture:** Matthew 12:46–50 | Luke 14:25–26 | John 15 | Romans 7:4
  1 Corinthians 7:32–33 | 2 Corinthians 4:17 | Ephesians 5:32 | Philippians 1:21
  Colossians 1:15–20 | Revelation 19:6–9; 21:4, 9–11

- **Read:** Chapter 7 of *The Relational God*

- **Preparation:**
  - Does thinking about what we studied concerning abiding in John 15 during Session 3 (p. 15) help clarify your thinking on this topic?
  - After reading Ephesians 5:22–32, meditate and pray over what Christ may be attempting to do in your life:
    - Are you honoring Christ's sacrifice (giving Himself up for you)?
    - What areas of your life is Christ identifying as areas for growth (sanctification)?
    - Are you in the Word? Are you letting it wash and cleanse you?
    - Are you pursuing holiness?

- **Intro Question(s):** Whether you had a big wedding or a small ceremony with a justice of the peace, what stands out to you about that day?

- **Teaching Outline**
  - Christ and the Church (Love and Submission)
    - **What is Christ's and our role in this now?** Christ's death and resurrection provides us with hope in the future. When we focus on this, our present suffering dissipates in light of the future glory:
      - **Philippians 1:21** – Paul can say for me to live is Christ and to die is gain.
      - **II Corinthians 4:17** – our present status is merely light and momentary affliction.
    - **What is Christ's and our role in this in the future?**
      - **Revelation 19:6–9; 21:9–11** – Christ and the church are now one
      - **Revelation 21:4** – Intimacy is the source of this love that Christ has for the church. But **from what unity does this love emanate?** The Godhead.
  - The Godhead (Intimacy)
    - **Ephesians 5:32** – the Trinity
    - **Colossians 1:15–20** shows **the difference between Christ and Adam.**
      - Adam made *in* the image of God
      - Christ *is* the image of God
    - Marriage reflects a more accurate picture of Christ
    - **John 15** – emphasize *abiding* leading to *bearing fruit*
    - **Romans 7:4** (1–6 is context) – links the concepts between law and grace (bearing fruit)
  - The Spiritual Covenant (Faithfulness and Leaving)
    - **Additionally, what is our role in this now?**
      - Local Church – **Matthew 12:46–50 and Luke 14:25–26**
      - Singleness – **1 Corinthians 7:32–33** – whereas marriage is a physical picture of a spiritual reality, **singleness blends the physical picture *with* the spiritual reality**, because their devotion to Christ can be undivided by anxiety about worldly things and pleasing a spouse.
  - The Other Commands:
    - Love (*agape*) encompasses gentleness, understanding, and honor
    - Love (*philos*) encompasses self-control, purity, keeping the home, and kindness
- **Conclusion:** God created marriage to provide a picture of His relationship with the church. Our love for each other and submission to each other are a picture of Christ's relationship to the church. Our intimacy is a picture of the oneness

and unity of the Godhead, and our faithfulness and leaving childhood are a picture of the spiritual covenant God makes with Abraham and fulfills in Christ—and, by extension, us. Singleness, too, when lived with "undivided devotion" to Christ, paints a picture of the final reality when we will all be united with Christ as one bride.

- **Additional Time? Pray for One Another, Plan Service Project, Fellowship!**

- **Digging Deeper and Additional Resources for Sessions 4, 5, and 6:**
  - Do a word study on "submission" or "love." Do you come to the same conclusions? Why or why not? Word studies used to be much more difficult and you needed specialized hermeneutical tools to complete them. Now, however, they are much easier. If you have never done a word study, I would encourage you to use either Blue Letter Bible online[1] (much easier and more intuitive for beginners) or the Logos Bible Software[2] (requires a download and you'll probably need to take one of their Introduction Courses). I am going to provide step-by-step instructions for using Blue Letter Bible[3]:
    1. After you access their main website, there's a section titled "Search the Bible." Type "Ephesians 5:22" into that search box.
    2. It will probably bring up all of Ephesians 5, separated by verse number. Click on "Eph 5:22."
    3. Now you will see Ephesians 5:22 in Greek, followed by what each word means in Greek **and** English. Click on the Greek reference for the word "submit yourselves" (G5293).
    4. Now you will see a screen that provides *a lot* of information about that specific word. Read through it. Click on the information that is interesting. Really dive into the word and where it is used in Scripture.
    5. Now do the same thing for "love" in Ephesians 5:25.

---

[1] https://www.blueletterbible.org/
[2] https://www.logos.com/
[3] This information can quickly become dated; however, the point is to teach you how to do a word study. If you find these instructions no longer applicable, Google "how to do a biblical word study" or go ask your pastor.

- Interview someone who has been married for 50 years or more.
- Read Larry McCall's book, *Loving Your Wife as Christ Loves the Church*.
- Read Robertson McQuilkin's book, *A Promise Kept*
- Read the Song of Solomon in the Bible (even better . . . read it out-loud with your spouse).
- Take Tommy Nelson's course *The Song of Solomon – a Study of Love, Sex, Marriage and Romance* or read his book *The Book of Romance: What Solomon Says About Love, Sex, and Intimacy*
- Listen to Timothy Keller's sermon series entitled "Marriage" (https://www.gospelinlife.com/marriage) or read his book *The Meaning of Marriage: Facing the Complexities of Commitment with the Wisdom of God*
- Watch *Fiddler on the Roof* and discuss the concept of love contained in the movie with your spouse.
- Take the 40-day *Love Dare* challenge by Alex and Stephen Kendrick (with or without your spouse).
- Take a study from Authentic Manhood (https://www.authenticmanhood.com) and/or get involved in an F3 group (https://f3nation.com/)
- Read the book of Hosea in the Bible
- Read Peter Kreeft's article "Sexual Symbolism" or listen to his lecture on the same topic http://peterkreeft.com/topics-more/sexual-symbolism.htm
- Do a word study on the word translated "mystery" in Ephesians 5:32. There may be more there than meets the eye (see p. 16 for more information on how to do a word study).
- Consider taking a spiritual gifts assessment. Ask your pastor to help you find one that is reputable.
- Read Gina Dalfonzo's book *One by One: Welcoming the Singles in Your Church*

Final Page(s) for Sketching, Doodling, or Additional Thoughts / Notes

Final Page(s) for Sketching, Doodling, or Additional Thoughts / Notes

Session 7 – How to Be a Sibling

- **Bridge:** We have examined how we *approach* God (as children) and how we *interact* with God individually and corporately as the church (like a spouse). Now it is time to consider how we *relate* to God through our relationships with one another as brothers and sisters in and through Christ.

- **Big Idea:** We are brothers and sisters in Christ and with Christ; therefore, we are commanded to treat each other in certain ways.

- **Key Scripture:** Matthew 7:3–5 | Mark 10:29–30 | Romans 1:11–13; 8:14–17, 29; 15:25–30; 16:14 | 2 Thessalonians 3:15 | Hebrews 2:5–3:6
  1 John 2:9–11; 3:10–12, 13–16; 4:20–21

- **Read:** Chapters 8 and 9 of *The Relational God*

- **Preparation:**
    o Read Romans 8:14–17, 29, then read Hebrews 2:5–3:6. Write a summary of the Hebrews passage.
    o Do you have siblings? Consider calling or meeting with one of them this week for the sole purpose of talking about your sibling relationship. If you don't have siblings, consider speaking with someone who does about their relationship with their brothers and sisters.

- **Intro Question(s)**
    o How many of you have or had siblings?
    o What characterized your relationship with your siblings?
    o How has that relationship changed as you've gotten older?

The Relational God Bible Study Leader's Guide

- **Teaching Outline**
  - **Hebrews 2:5–3:6 (what three points should we take from this passage)**
    1. We are brothers and sisters with Christ (v. 10–11)
    2. That was God's plan from the beginning (He both made the plan and executed the plan) – v. 8–13
       - We are to be rulers with God, but in order for that to happen we have to be perfected.
       - God accomplishes that perfection through Christ (He is the only one who is perfected – and therefore honored and glorified)
       - Through this He provides the comfort of empathy for suffering *and* the final solution for that suffering. He is the High Priest *and* the ultimate sacrifice.
    3. We are fellow heirs with Christ (v. 5–8)
  - **Mark 10:29–30** shows us another truth
    - According to the Hebrews passage, we are brothers and sisters *with* Christ (vertical)
    - According to the Mark passage, we are brothers and sisters *in* Christ (horizontal)
    - Through these two passages, we learn **the two different types of sibling relationships which Christ establishes through His work on the cross and resurrection from the dead**
  - So now that we have established the theological side of this coin, let's look at the practical side. How are we to treat our brothers and sisters in Christ?
    - In order to do that, I looked up the word *adelphos* in the New Testament
    - **It is used 346 times and it is used to reference the following three relationships: a physical brother, a natural brother, or a spiritual brother.**

- - - When referencing spiritual "brothers" there are three categories that were helpful:
        1. A direct spiritual command, using our relationship to one another "as brothers" as the rationale (i.e. do this *because* this is how siblings treat one another).
        2. A command or idea that is repeated many times (i.e. it so typifies sibling relationships that it is the only proper interpretation).
        3. A command or idea referencing an earthly sibling group (i.e. it is apparent that siblings out – or ought not – to treat each other this way).
  - **What are the commands to our brothers and sisters *in Christ* based on these three categories?**
      - Warnings: 2 Thessalonians 3:15
      - Unifying Love through Peace, Reconciliation, and Eschewing Sinful Anger: 1 John 2:9–11; 3:10–16; 4:20–21
      - Greeting, Visiting, and Keeping Their Company: Romans 1:11–13; 16:14
      - Supporting and Praying for Them: Romans 15:25–30
      - Being Equitable: Matthew 7:3–5
      - Misc. Commands:
          - Forgiving One Another
          - Strengthening One Another
          - Comforting and Encouraging One Another
          - Encouraging One Another in Purity
  - **Can we extrapolate those same commands to our physical brothers and sisters?**
      - God's Word contains imperatives for our relationship with one another in the body of Christ, but the inference from Scripture is strong that they should characterize our relationship with our physical brothers and sisters, as well. Regardless of whether you acknowledge the inference, I would challenge you that it couldn't hurt. It would not be detrimental for us to treat our physical siblings in the ways described above.
      - We must always keep in mind, though, that our spiritual family is the real and lasting family. When our physical family is also part of our spiritual family, then all the better.
- **Conclusion:** God uses our relationships with our brothers and sisters to provide unique insight into how we should be treating one another in the body of Christ.

The Relational God Bible Study Leader's Guide

- **Additional Time? Pray for One Another, Plan a Service Project, Fellowship!**

- **Digging Deeper and Additional Resources for Session 7:**
    - Do a word study on *adelphos* (see p. 16 for more information on how to do a word study). Do you come up with the same results? How else might you categorize the usage of *brother* in the New Testament? If you really want a stretch, after you do that, find the Hebrew word for *brother* and do the same word study in the Old Testament. What did you find?
    - Ask your siblings or close Christian friends to rate you on the six commands (1 to 6). Use that to start a discussion about where you could improve (don't get defensive).
    - Read Jeffrey Kluger's *Times* special on Siblings, or (slightly easier) watch his TED Talk on Siblings (https://www.ted.com/talks/jeffrey_kluger_the_sibling_bond). What spiritual correlations can you make?

Final Page(s) for Sketching, Doodling, or Additional Thoughts / Notes

Final Page(s) for Sketching, Doodling, or Additional Thoughts / Notes

Session 8 – How to Be a Parent

- **Bridge:** We have examined how we *approach* God (as children), how we *interact* with God individually and corporately as the church (like a spouse), and how we *relate* to God through our relationships with one another as brothers and sisters in and through Christ. Now we will examine how God **approaches**, **interacts with**, and **relates to us** by examining what the Scripture has to say to parents.

- **Big Idea:** Parents are commanded to teach and discipline their children. Fathers specifically are commanded to be gentle with their children. Mothers specifically are commanded to love their children.

- **Key Scripture:** Deuteronomy 6:1–9 | Proverbs 13:24; 15:1; 19:18 | Ephesians 6:4 Colossians 3:21 | Titus 2:4 | Hebrews 12:11

- **Read:** Chapters 10 and 11 of *The Relational God*

- **Preparation:**
    - Review the section on "Discipline" from Session 3 ("Sons and Daughters of God"). How does that help inform what your role ought to be as a parent?
    - Think about the best teacher you ever had. What did he or she do that made them great?

- **Intro Question(s)**
    - If you were given the choice to have your children experience life in the same way that you experienced it as a child, would you make such a choice?
    - What is the most frustrating thing you see about yourself in your own children? What do you wish someone would have told you about that when you were younger?
    - How many of us want self-parenting kids?
    - Do you remember the three commands to children? [honor; obey; learn]
    - **What three things do you think parents are commanded to do in Scripture (as a father or as a mother)?** – Teach and Model | Discipline | Fathers – Gentle | Mothers – Love

- **Teaching Outline**
  - Teach and Model
    - **Deuteronomy 6:1–9**
      - v. 1 – "teach" = *lamad*
        - used 86 times in OT
        - translated "teach," "learn," or "instruct" 81 of those times
      - v. 7 – "teach" = *shaman*
        - used 9 times in OT
        - all other times it is indicative of how deadly a weapon is ("whetting" a sword; "sharpening" an arrow/tongue).
          - Why do you sharpen a weapon? [insure effectiveness]
          - How is weapon sharpened? [through repetition]
    - **What is the best way to learn something?** Author of Deuteronomy is commanded to "teach," so he tells the people to "teach" them. To repeat them. To sharpen their children with them. *Teaching is just as much for the parents as it is for the children.*
    - **How should we be teaching our children? What is the purpose of teaching our children (particularly considering what we discovered was the goal of childhood in session 1)?** We build monuments (vv. 7–9). We repeat. The goal is to shift the dependence of our children off of us and onto God. *We need to be using every physical opportunity to repeat the good news of the nature and character of God to our children!*
    - This is about the heart and not about behaviors.
  - Discipline
    - **What is the purpose of discipline? How should discipline be used?**
      - Discipline, when properly understood, is an extension of teaching. It is teaching with consequences.
      - Do you remember the word in Hebrews for "discipline"? It was *paideuō*. There's a reason "disciple" is at the root of the word "discipline."
      - Discipline is focused training.

- Corporal Punishment:
  - Only 4x Scriptures reference striking a child (for discipline – Proverbs 13:24; 22:15; 23:13; and 29:15), and only 1x Scripture (Proverbs 23:13) actually *prescribes* striking your child.
  - All these Scriptures reference *the rod*. The guidelines seem to be:
    - Correction
    - Driving folly from the heart of a child
    - Salvation from the path of destruction
  - The broadest of these is "folly," and this word only appears in Psalms and Proverbs. It is employed in the following three specific contexts:
    - Wrongdoing
    - The opposite of knowledge and good sense
    - Anger
- Therefore, *teaching and modeling* in a general sense (through the use of memorials); *disciplining by teaching with consequences*; and *disciplining through physical course corrections* are three tools God Himself uses with us. He additionally gives them to us for our children. The purpose is for capturing the hearts of our children. So now we need to consider the attitude in which we teach and discipline.

- **Gentleness (Fathers) – Fathers, what does it mean to not be harsh with your children?**
  - **Ephesians 6:1–4**
  - Think of **Proverbs 15:1**. The opposite of wrath is gentleness.
  - **Why is this particular command given to fathers?** Remember in Session 4 when I said that the curse can be posited from a male perspective as the husband ruling over the wife—taking advantage of her desire—or, from a female perspective, as the wife desiring the role of the husband—being disappointed in his leadership. The sin for wives is a lack of submission. The sin for husbands is authoritarian rule. So, too, over other aspects of the home.
  - **Hebrews 12:11** – this is what discipline should yield. So, what characterizes your household? Anger (**Ephesians 6:4**) and discouragement (**Colossians 3:21**) or the peaceful fruit of righteousness?

- **Love (Mothers) – Mothers, what sort of love should you provide to your children? How is that different than the love we have discussed up to this point in the study?**
    - **Titus 2:4–5:** Two reasons this type of love is specified
        1. The word used is *philoteknos*. It is different from the *agape* love commanded of husbands for their wives. It is not unconditional. It is practical.
            - **How does this love compare to the commands we saw to siblings in last session's study?** Brotherly sort of love [and their opposites]: warnings [blissful ignorance], unifying love through peace, reconciliation, and eschewing sinful anger [divisiveness and anger]; greeting, visiting, and keeping their company [selfishness with time]; supporting and praying for them [selfishness with resources and a lack of spiritual concern]; being equitable [playing favorites]; forgiving, comforting, and encouraging in purity [walking in unforgiveness, hardness, and cowardice, and with impurity].
            - Funny, these are almost the exact things Titus mentions: self-controlled [eschewing sinful anger and being equitable]; pure [forgiving, comforting, and with purity]; working at home [greeting; visiting; keeping their company; and supporting and praying for them]; kind [unifying love through peace, reconciliation, and eschewing sinful anger]
        2. It is tangible, but it is not natural (it must be taught)
    - **Why is this particular command given to mothers?** As we just identified, many of the commands directed to one specific role are likely relate to that role's specific challenge from the fall. The commands for wives and mothers drive toward unselfish, servant love, including not attempting to usurp the leadership from the husband over disappointment in his fulfillment (or lack of fulfillment) of that role.
- **Conclusion:** In Session 2, we examined how the role of the child is to "honor" and "obey." If we are teaching and modeling for our children, if we are disciplining with gentleness (fathers) and love (mothers), then our children will have an easier time of practicing honor and obedience according to the biblical imperative. Through that honor and obedience,

our children can eventually shift their dependence off us and onto Christ. The child's role is getting this right; the parents' role is facilitation. Often, children will choose to shift their dependence onto themselves, a lover, drugs, a career, or any myriad of things. Ultimately, though, all of our parenting should be directed toward getting our children's dependence off us and onto Christ. That is the purpose of parenting. To do this, our children need to see us exercise dependence upon the Lord as we help them, little by little, move from obedience to honor.

- **Additional Time? Pray for One Another, Plan a Service Project, Fellowship!**

Final Page(s) for Sketching, Doodling, or Additional Thoughts / Notes

Final Page(s) for Sketching, Doodling, or Additional Thoughts / Notes

Final Page(s) for Sketching, Doodling, or Additional Thoughts / Notes

Session 9 – Mother & Father Heart of God

- **Bridge:** In every other situation, the spiritual metaphor informed our relationship to God through Christ. *We* are the sons and daughters of God through Christ; *we* are the bride of Christ; *we* are brothers and sisters in and with Christ. For this metaphor, though, we will see how God **approaches**, **interacts with**, and **relates to** us – as a parent.

- **Big Idea:** As we grow in the Lord, we have the responsibility to be a spiritual parent. Our roles as both physical and spiritual parents reflect the mother and father heart of God.

- **Key Scripture:** Genesis 1:28; 17:5-6 | Matthew 6:9-13; 7:7-11; 28:19 | John 15
  Romans 8:15 | Colossians 1:15 | Titus 3:3-7 | Hebrews 12:5-11 | James 3:17-18
  Revelation 3:19

- **Read:** Chapter 12 of *The Relational God*

- **Preparation:**
    - Parenting can often be a source of deep angst and uncertainty. It can also be the source of tremendous joy and pride. Which do you think God wants you to feel? Which do you think God feels for you?
    - Think about where God is identified as "Father" in the Bible. Can you think of any Old Testament passages that identify him as such? Why do we think of God as a father?
    - Does thinking about "motherly" attributes of God make you uncomfortable? Why? Is your discomfort biblical?

- **Intro Question(s):**
    - How does our role as mothers and fathers reflect what we should be doing spiritually?
    - What about how God approaches us?

- **Teaching Outline**
  - Spiritual Reproduction: remember 1 John 2:13–14?
    - **What responsibility do we have to advance the kingdom of God through making disciples?**
    - The initial commands in Genesis are reflected in the Great Commission
      - **Genesis 1:28** – "be fruitful and multiply" and "fill the earth"
      - **Genesis 17:5-6** – "father of a multitude of nations"
      - **Matthew 28:19** – "go therefore and make disciples of all nations"
  - **How does God fulfill all the commands given to parents?**
    - Teaching / Modeling
      - God commands the people to "teach" them to their children
      - God provides models (some good, some bad)
        - He provides His Son (*the* image – not just *an* image – **Colossians 1:15**)
        - He does all these things—teaching, discipline, gentleness, and love—perfectly (thus modeling modeling)
    - Discipline
      - Mentoring (*paideuō*) – "reminders" through His Word (the word "reminders" is reminiscent of the story I tell in chapter 11); the Holy Spirit, and our brothers and sisters in Christ.
      - Corporeal – **Hebrews 12:5–11**
  - **What are the specific *fatherly* attributes which God demonstrates? How does that help you more fully understand His nature and character?**
    - God is constantly called "father" throughout the New Testament, but not much in the Old Testament.
    - It is Christ who really introduces Him as such.
      - Lord's Prayer – **Matthew 6:9–13**
      - **John 15** (vinedresser)
      - **Romans 8:15** and Galatians 4:6 – "Abba! Father!"
    - The fatherly attribute of gentleness is seen of God in OT (2 Samuel 22:36; Psalm 18:35; Isaiah 40:11), and of Christ in NT (Matthew 11:29–30)
    - The wisdom from above in **James 3:17** (and what does it yield in **v. 18**)?
    - Think about a parent in regard to prayer (**Matthew 7:7–11**)

- o **What are the specific *motherly* attributes which God demonstrates? How does that help you more fully understand His nature and character?**
    - Jesus "loves" (in the *philos*) sort of way
        - For sinners and tax collectors: Matthew 11:19 and Luke 7:34.
        - For us (**John 15:12–16** – *friends*)
    - Jesus has this love for us, because God has this love for Him (John 5:20), and therefore for us (John 16:26–27).
    - **How do we see Christ demonstrate the *philos* love that is attributed to mothers in the Titus passage we covered last session?**
        - It is Christ who authorizes us to receive this love from God (**Titus 3:3–7**).
        - **Revelation 3:19** – this type of love encapsulates the other two aspects of parenting (teaching and discipline).
    - Other "feminine" characteristics:
        - God births and nurses
        - God cares for others (maternally)
        - God is a homemaker

- **Additional Time? Pray for One Another, Plan a Service Project, Fellowship!**

- **Digging Deeper and Additional Resources for Sessions 8 and 9:**
    - o Participate in Paul David Tripp's video-based *Getting to the Heart of Parenting* conference or read his book *Parenting: 14 Gospel Principles that Can Radically Change Your Family*.
    - o Read Jason Helopoulos' book *A Neglected Grace: Family Worship in the Christian Home*. If possible, work through this book in a small group with whom you can discuss implementing the concepts of the book in your family.
    - o Read C.S. Lewis' book *The Four Loves*.
    - o There are many issues that we face as parents about which there are no specific commands in Scripture. Choose an issue and think about it from the framework we have been discussing (teaching, discipline, gentleness, and love). Perhaps choose a good book that would apply a biblical framework to one of these issues (for instance, if you are concerned

about how to think biblically about parenting and the technology that your children are consuming, you may want to read *The Tech-Wise Family* by Andy Crouch).
- There are a lot of really BIG concepts in this section. Consider partnering with another mature believer in your church to study some of these concepts further:
  - Spiritual parenting / Discipleship
  - Fathers and God as father
  - Mothers and the mother heart of God

  Additional study might mean searching the Scripture for those concepts, reading more books (with concepts like this, it is always helpful to start with recognized theology books and branch out from there), looking at how the historical church understood the concept (look at creeds, confessions, and catechisms). There are some established methods for doing a study like this, and there are also some ways that can lead down unhelpful paths (for instance, doing a Google search on "the mother heart of God" or even "God the Father" can quickly lead down the road to heresy). Partnering with your community and other strong believers will help you be both thorough and orthodox in such a study.

- Read Millard Erickson's *God the Father Almighty: A Contemporary Exploration of Divine Attributes*, and/or A.W. Tozer's *The Attributes of God Volume 1: A Journey into the Father's Heart* and/or *The Attributes of God Volume 2: Deeper into the Father's Heart*.
- Read Dallas Willard's *The Great Omission: Reclaiming Jesus's Essential Teaching on Discipleship*, and/or Francis Chan's *Multiply: Disciples Making Disciples*, and/or A.W. Tozer's *Discipleship: What Truly Means to Be a Christian—Collected Insights from A.W. Tozer*.
- Read Jen Pollock Michel's *Keeping Place: Reflections on the Meaning of Home* and/or Tish Harrison Warren's *Liturgy of the Ordinary: Sacred Practices in Everyday Life*.

Final Page(s) for Sketching, Doodling, or Additional Thoughts / Notes

Final Page(s) for Sketching, Doodling, or Additional Thoughts / Notes

Session 10 – Adoption and Conclusion

- **Bridge:** Everything we have been talking about is ours through Christ, but it is only ours because God chooses to adopt us into it. We are not born into God's home, yet we long for it. This is the point. This is what we have been building up to. Our relationships—when conducted properly—point to the ultimate culmination and final rest at home. By adoption into God's family—through Christ—we receive everything about which we have been studying over the past few sessions. Our earthly family relationships are dim reflections of this spiritual reality. The closer we follow the commands governing those familial relationships, the more accurately and beautifully they reflect the ideal of the spiritual reality. And the spiritual reality is that we are adopted as sons and daughters of God by being fellow heirs with Christ, who is the firstborn among many brothers. Collectively, this is consummated into an everlasting covenant at the end of time for the purpose of ruling together with Christ in His eternal kingdom! Outside of our adoption into this spiritual family through Christ, we have no hope.

- **Big Idea:** It is only through adoption that we are able to be part of God's family. Adoption is the finishing touch on the masterpiece of a metaphor that God has breathed into His creation. Look to your relationships. Where you have problems interpersonally, you may discover those same tendencies to be thorny areas spiritually.

- **Key Scripture:** Romans 8:14–17 | Galatians 4:4–7 | Ephesians 1:3–10; 5–6:4

- **Read:** Conclusion and Afterword of *The Relational God*

- **Preparation:**
    - Go back over the content. What has been meaningful to you?
    - Consider sharing how you have been personally affected by the study.

- **Intro Question(s):**
    - To whom have all these relationships pointed? Support the answer.
    - How many of you have been touched in some way by adoption?

- **Teaching Outline**
  - **Introduction: Ryan Jon video** (https://www.youtube.com/watch?v=E_Zy3kQr-0w)
    - **How is spiritual adoption different from physical adoption?**
      - Adoption in our context often comes with a lot of uncertainty.
      - The angst is due to a lack of context. But in spiritual adoption, we know the context. **[And this is where we see what is the role of Christ in our adoption as sons and daughters of God?]**
        - 1 Corinthians 6:9–11 (such were some of you)
        - Luke 16:19–31 (rich man and Lazarus)
          - Jesus ends the story by alluding to Himself.
          - Remember Hebrews 2? Moses merely pointed to Jesus
          - He is the heir
          - He decides to share that with us.
    - Yet whenever the Bible speaks of adoption, it does so in context of *gain*. Adoption in the Bible is typically pictured as rescue (gaining life) or inheritance (gaining wealth).
  - **How do the Old Testament and New Testament concepts of adoption differ?**
    - Old Testament
      - Almost all the Old Testament reference to adoption pertain to rescue (gaining life).
      - The Hebrew language does not really have a word for adoption, so most references to adoption in the Old Testament have to do with rescue or gaining life (Genesis 48:5–6; Exodus 2:10, 4:22–23; 2 Samuel 7:14; Esther 2:7; Jeremiah 31:8–9; Hosea 11:1).
    - New Testament
      - The Greco-Roman societies have this concept of adoption, but it is almost entirely about inheritance – legally.
      - Thus, in the New Testament, the Hebrew sense of rescue (gaining life) is often mingled with the Greco-Roman sense of inheritance or gaining wealth (Romans 8:14–23; 2 Corinthians 6:17–18; Galatians 3:26; 4:4–7; Ephesians 1:5; 1 John 3:1–2).
      - Anyone want to take a stab at what adoption is often contrasted with? [slavery]
      - Let's look at **Romans 8:14–17**

- How does the idea of adoption in Christ synthesize these two concepts?
  - We receive *rescue* from slavery and eternal death
  - We receive abiding intimacy with the Father
  - We receive a new family (worshiping unit)
  - We receive the inheritance (now . . . not when someone dies)
- **Review**
  - **What are the three primary commands for children?**
    - Honor
    - Obey
    - Learn
  - **Where could you personally improve in your relationship as a child (spiritually or physically)?** Personal story
  - **What are the seven primary commands for marriage?**
    - Husbands:
      - Love
      - Gentleness, Understanding, and Honor
      - Leave and Hold Fast
    - Wives:
      - Submit
      - Self-controlled, pure, working at home, and kind
    - Physical Intimacy
    - Faithfulness
  - **Where could you personally improve in your relationship as a spouse (spiritually or physically).** Personal story
  - **What are the eight commands in Scripture about how we should treat our brothers and sisters (in Christ)?**
    - Warnings
    - Unifying Love through Peace, Reconciliation, and Eschewing Sinful Anger
    - Greeting, Visiting, and Keeping Their Company
    - Supporting and Praying for Them
    - Being Equitable
    - Misc. Commands:
      - Forgiving One Another
      - Strengthening One Another
      - Comforting and Encouraging One Another
      - Encouraging One Another in Purity
  - **Where could you personally improve in your relationship as a sibling (spiritually or physically)?** Personal story

The Relational God Bible Study Leader's Guide

- - - **What are the four primary commands for parents?**
      - Teaching
      - Discipline
      - Fathers: Gentleness
      - Mothers: Love
    - **Where could you personally improve in your relationship as a parent (spiritually or physically)?** Personal story
    - **How does your status as an adopted son or daughter of God change your outlook on your position in the family of God?**

- **Digging Deeper and Additional Resources for Session 10:**
    - Do a word study on *huiothesia* (see p. 16 for more information on how to do a word study). If you want to dive even deeper, try to find the concept of adoption in the Old Testament and record what you discover.
    - Interview someone who has been adopted (and is willing and open to speaking about it). How does their experience support or challenge the content from this study?
    - Read *Sons in the Son* by David B Gardner

Final Page(s) for Sketching, Doodling, or Additional Thoughts / Notes

Final Page(s) for Sketching, Doodling, or Additional Thoughts / Notes

Additional Page(s) for sketching, doodling, or additional thoughts / notes

Additional Page(s) for Sketching, Doodling, or Additional Thoughts / Notes

Additional Page(s) for Sketching, Doodling, or Additional Thoughts / Notes

Additional Page(s) for Sketching, Doodling, or Additional Thoughts / Notes

Additional Page(s) for Sketching, Doodling, or Additional Thoughts / Notes

Additional Page(s) for Sketching, Doodling, or Additional Thoughts / Notes

www.ingramcontent.com/pod-product-compliance
Lightning Source LLC
Chambersburg PA
CBHW041434010526
44118CB00002B/66